THE
DARK
TUNNEL
I WALKED DOWN

Spiderwize
Remus House
Coltsfoot Drive
Woodston
Peterborough
PE2 9BF

www.spiderwize.com

A CIP catalogue record for this book is available from the British Library.

The views expressed in this work are solely those of the author and do not
necessarily reflect the views of the publisher, and the publisher hereby
disclaims any responsibility for them.

ISBN: 978-1-912694-56-3

eBook ISBN: 978-1-912694-57-0

THE DARK TUNNEL
I WALKED DOWN

MARYANN LAURENCE

SPIDERWIZE
Peterborough UK
2018

Dedicated with love to those I call family,
without you my life would be empty.
xxx

And to Dr Alison Beveridge,
thank you for believing me.

Some names and places have been altered.

If you're going through a tough time don't fight it on your own, go and get professional help.

The four books make up -

FOUR SEASONS IN SALLY'S LIFE.

In reading order, they are -

THE RELUCTANT MUM

IT'S POSITIVE: TAKE TWO

THE DARK TUNNEL I WALKED DOWN

IT'S LIKE THE MARRIAGE NEVER HAPPENED

www. folded-corner.weebly.com

Season Three Was A Dark And Lonely Time

Although this is a short book, for me it was a long journey.

I'd like to tell you that this is a work of fiction, but it's not.

The depression was like a long dark tunnel that had built itself around me, it closed in on me cutting off the light. No one and nothing was coming to my rescue.

The long days of winter were getting to me, I'd had these feelings before as I'd had the famous Baby Blues after giving birth to Anna, my first child. Sometimes I think that as Anna had been unplanned, the loss of freedom, together with my loss of independence (and salary!) culminated in a depression that lasted an awfully long time. But this time it seems the Baby Blues has turned into the Black Dog of depression, it hounds me night and day. Plus, it's taking longer than I expected to find the right medication for it – I never knew there were so many pills! It seemed to drag on for months. Some of the pills made me feel as if I was floating to the ceiling and spaced out, or I'd have long bouts of sleeping and I'd get lost if I drove anywhere. I'd go shopping and come back with nothing, it was a relief when we eventually found the right one.

Postnatal Depression (PND) they call it – how long is it supposed to hang around? I'd managed to come off the pills quite quickly last time, but the depression didn't go away, not really, I only fooled myself (and everyone around me) into thinking it had.

But it came back with a vengeance soon after the birth of my second child, James. I searched the internet and found a website for struggling mums and I was encouraged when I read it. So, I steeled myself and made an appointment to see a GP to talk about my depression.

The GP leant forward a little on his desk, balanced on one elbow and looked at me in a 'pat-pat there-there' manner as he told me that his wife had given birth a week before I had, and that she didn't have depression, so I hadn't got it!

I came away from the GP deflated. I'd had to be very brave to go and 'confess' that I was a depressed mum – I sobbed in the loneliness I called home.

A few days later Kirsty, my health visitor, came to see how things were going with me and James and I told her what had happened with the GP, she was furious! She said I should have been prescribed medication after this birth as a precaution because the depression I'd had previously had been so bad. I'm not sure if this is normal practice or if she was just trying to cheer me up. So, I booked myself in to see a different doctor, this time it was the lady GP I had seen while I was pregnant with James; she's a working mum as well and she understood the guilt I experienced over leaving Anna when I went back to work, as well as the struggles I was going through now. My guilt over Anna was because when she was about six months she had been in nursery and I was back working full time. I missed too many milestones of her young life, and now she had a baby brother to share what little time she had with me. I always felt she had the short straw, and this working-mum-guilt added to the depression I was experiencing.

Ian, my hubby, persuaded me to sell my car early in the marriage, so he could put his car in the garage, this made it difficult for me and the kids to go anywhere. I think the loss of my own car added to my loss of independence and social isolation. Before I was married I'd had my own home, car and holidays, but there is none of that left now, it all seems like a dream and in stark contrast to the life I now live.

Over the past few months I believed I was the only person in the world with depression; I felt it was something I should be ashamed of. People would TELL ME to 'cheer up!' and 'look at your two lovely children!' But I couldn't cheer up. I was sure there was no one feeling as bad as me, and what was more, no one was prepared to listen and take me seriously. The depression was like a very dark long tunnel that had built itself around me, it closed in on me, cutting off the light. No one and nothing was coming to my rescue. And it was only me. I was a failure for having this depression.

A failure for succumbing to it.

A failed mum.

I now had two children and they needed me, and a husband, to whom I was becoming irrelevant, so he sort-of needed me to keep paying the bills. Well he had a job and was busy swimming or walking the hills at weekends and going out with his pals in the week, so we didn't see much of him.

This meant I was the problem. I'd tell myself off for being weak, and I'd shout at myself! I needed to pull myself together! Be who they needed me to be, didn't I know that! What was I doing wallowing in self-pity? There were lots of women worse off than me, look at them, they're not depressed, they have proper illnesses!

For some reason the medication I took last time wasn't suiting me, so I went along to a few appointments with the lady GP and she would monitor how I was doing, she wanted to make sure the medication was the right one and the right strength, and that I was eating and sleeping properly – this seemed to take ages as there are loads of meds for depression, I'm not sure exactly how long it took, but thank goodness we got there in the end.

Ian meanwhile would expect the four of us to go out visiting his family and friends. I never really got on with them, they'd tolerate me, and I'd tolerate them; it was here I learned to be good at pretending everything was fine and at playing 'happy families.' I'd go along feeling hollow, a living breathing shell. I was withdrawing from everything and everyone, except the children. The children became my focus for living. My rays of sunlight were times spent with them.

At one appointment my GP asked how I felt about joining a small support group for women with postnatal depression, I didn't know they existed. She gave me the contact details and I said it might be ok to give it a try. It was scheduled to last for seven weeks - who ever thought depression only lasts for seven weeks should try living with it!

I went along and found a lovely group of women, I was the oldest and really felt my age. My baggage of problems included having a less than supportive husband, a young baby, and youngster at the school nursery, plus I'd still got severe pain in my pelvis, this had become a continuous struggle as it had come on during my pregnancy, and on top of this there was the depression; I was taking a mixture of medication just to face the world.

The group was run by two support workers, they were lovely and patient, they gently led the discussions and gave us hope. Our names were written on an old board, which for me for the first time in a long time, symbolised self-worth. I belonged here, I had a place here, I was accepted, depression and all.

We had our babies with us and it was good to see James play happily on the floor with the baby toys, he particularly loved playing with the 'multi-gym,' Ian refused to buy one – he'd refused to buy a stairgate until Anna tumbled from top to bottom, I wasn't allowed to buy things without his permission; he held the purse strings very tight.

Ian knew I was depressed and that I was going to what he called a 'depressed women's group' but he didn't ask about it. He had far too much to say when he got home from work, telling me all about his working day, where he'd been, as well as who and what he'd seen, and for the rest of the evening he would stretch out on the settee and watch his TV programmes.

While I was at the women's group Anna was safely in the school nursery for the morning, this meant I could sit for a couple of hours with a small group of women who were going through the same as I was. This was such a supportive time for me.

It was good to go along to the group once a week to drink coffee, talk about the baby, the lack of sleep, the family, the older children, and for some of us the re-occurring depression. I found it helped to talk about the medication and the side effects as it helped me understand it better. Many of us were working hard to come off the meds, a bit at a time, and we supported each other through this, celebrating when someone had successfully reduced their medication level.

Some of the women had gone through IVF to conceive their baby and they'd paid thousands of pounds. The women and their babies were healthy, but depression had set in and some of their family members were being unsupportive saying 'You wanted the baby, you paid for it, you get on with it,' as if that's going to help.

The group was scheduled to meet for seven weeks, but for week seven I had a check-up appointment for James, so I wouldn't be able to go to the last session, but I reasoned I was doing ok as I was slowly reducing the medication and I was excited to take James for his check-up as he was doing really well.

Then on week five, the group was told that next week (week six) we would have a visiting speaker. This sounded ok, but I was a little sad because for me week six was going to be my last session.

The day of the support group came around and we sat waiting for our visiting speaker. She turned up late, not a good start because the sessions were only two hours long; in she bounded like a healthy PE teacher, jolly hockey sticks and all! She didn't waste time learning our names nor anything about us and, board wiper in hand with her back to the group, she asked if it was OK to clean off the board. The group seemed to take a collective breath in! I felt physical pain, as if something precious was being ripped away from me, and I blurted out 'No, you can't rub that off, that's our name board.' She looked round, and seemed stunned that someone had dared to say no.

But this didn't put her off her stride and she proceeded to whizz through a brief introduction and dived into a well-rehearsed tirade about the drugs we were taking and telling us how we couldn't possibly come off them because we needed them so much we'd probably be on them for years. I felt very hurt by her words. The whole group sat in stunned silence. She went on and on about this drug and that drug and that we couldn't ever come off them.

At one point James needed his nappy seeing to, so I changed him on the unit in the corner of the room, doing this meant I had my back to the group and the visitor. One of the support workers was close by and, whispering, asked me if I was OK, I was obviously displaying signs of not being OK. I sort-of nodded while I finished seeing to James. I made sure he was happy and put him back down to play. The group were still sitting in silence while the visitor droned on and on.

I could feel myself getting more and more up-tight about what she was saying until finally I snapped. I said to her 'You've come in here to a group that's been meeting for weeks, you turned up late and you've hardly told us your name or why you're here, you've taken no interest in finding out our names nor our situations. You want to rub off the name board that has grown as the group has grown and now you are banging on about us not coming off the medication. Well I for one am working hard at coming off the damn pills and I'm winning the battle, it's slow but I'm getting there, and it won't be because of anything you've said but because of the support and acceptance I've found here in this group.

I've been supported by these women week in and week out. This is my final session because I can't come next week and you're spoiling it.' Then I shut up. And so did she. She sat down and looked quite shocked. And the support workers took over what remained of the session, but it was too late for me because as lunchtime was approaching I had to leave to fetch Anna. I'd never in my life spoken like that to anyone. I was shaken by my out-of-character out-burst.

Seven weeks is not long enough for support groups. Depression, and indeed any mental illness, can last much longer than that and support needs to be in place for the whole time, and for the times it comes back. Information needs to be freely and readily available, whether it's books, webpages, specialists to talk to or groups to go to, but the support needs to be there.

On reflection, when I went to the doctors the first time and he didn't believe me, I felt like a child that had dropped an ice cream and was being told off for getting something so simple so very wrong. This was a truly dreadful experience, I could easily have spiralled further into my depressed state. Doctors and professionals need to listen to their patients.

It was being believed that gave me hope and helped me find my way out of the dark tunnel. It was a slow process but eventually I got there.

My health visitor, Kirsty, gave me hope. The lady GP did too, she patiently helped me find the right meds and told me about the support group.

The two workers and every woman at the group helped me more than I can say. This was what I needed. This is what got me through, it was people being there supporting me and being willing to listen, they gave me that precious gift, they gave me time. I needed to sit and have a coffee and have the freedom to cry without wearing a badge of shame.

Time went by don't ask me how, it just did. The Monday-Friday routine established itself, Ian would drive off to work and my mornings were busy getting two kids ready – then the three of us would get the bus and take Anna to the school nursery for the morning, and while she was there I'd 'do something' – often sitting in a local cafe having a coffee and feeding James, and then fetching Anna and we'd get the bus and go back home. Our afternoons consisted of having 'little lunch' as we called it, then a game or two, or drawing, reading, counting and colours and sometimes a bit of cooking. Then when Ian turned up it would be tea-time; I'd bath the children and settle them down for sleep and crawl to bed myself, exhausted from the strain of surviving another day. Ian of course would be watching his programs and woe betide anyone that interfered with his TV routine. He would only speak to me or the kids when the commercials were on.

Twice during this time I had a visit from someone, they would come around with the offer of helping me, but it would end up with them sitting in the lounge while I made cups of tea and got them biscuits. And then they'd go, and I'd be left alone to cope. No. Not alone, and not coping either. I didn't get any alone-time, I was either with Ian and the kids, or I was with the kids. Even if I was sitting on the toilet or in the bath, someone would feel it world-stoppingly-imperative to talk to me through the door, or to open the door a bit so they could be heard and be given priority over whatever I was doing. I was never allowed any peace nor quiet. The interruptions bombarded other areas of my life too.

I used to be in an orchestra but had to give it up because Ian made it difficult for me to go. It used to be that on orchestra days (Saturdays) Helen would drive to our house for about noon and I would drive us to rehearsal or concert. But Ian changed his shopping habit and decided he wanted to go shopping on Saturday mornings, alone. Not a problem there you'd think. But when it was an orchestra Saturday he started getting home a bit later and a bit later, and he made it difficult for Helen and me to get there on time. So in the end I dropped out of orchestra. I dropped out because I couldn't face asking him to make sure he was home in time for me to go. I avoided confrontation, despite having been in the orchestra for 15 years. The sadness I experienced over this ran very deep, and in the following months I had to sell my instruments so I could pay for shopping. I also sold my jewellery to pay the bills. I seriously considered selling mums jewellery, but I couldn't part with it, I'd got so little left of who I was.

I considered declaring bankruptcy, and I know for some folk this is the option for them, but when I looked into it I could see it wasn't the option for me, so I decided that no matter what I would try my hardest not to go down that route.

Around this time I realised I had become the subject of whispered conversations between Ian, his family and his friends. I'd hear his responses 'she's not so good today / struggling sometimes / she's fine.' Conversations like this took place even with me in the room, as if I was invisible and I'd suddenly lost my hearing as well as my feelings. They'd talk quietly in a huddle and look at me from across the room. I felt as if my skin had broken out in an oozing smelly contagious rash, and that everyone was afraid to come near me in case they caught this disease called depression. I wanted to scream and shout at them for being so damn ignorant, but I couldn't, it was as if I hadn't got a voice, I couldn't speak up for myself anymore. A shadow of the woman I had been only a handful of years ago.

So no, I wasn't fine. This tunnel was dark and long, and I was very lonely. I felt isolated even if I was in a room full of people. I think my loneliness had come initially from my mom dying when I was in my teens, and dad dying a few years after that, and then my sister moved to work abroad. Growing up an orphan was tough. So when I got married I thought my loneliness was at an end, but I was wrong.

My friends seemed loathed to visit more than once or twice, they'd always say they were busy. Ian would dash to answer the front door when anyone knocked, and he'd stand at the top of the steps that led to the door, towering above everyone, enjoying his moment of perceived power, intimidating them even before they crossed the threshold. The atmosphere in the house had become cold, unwelcoming, and hostile, no wonder none of my friends wanted to visit. It was as if Ian was questioning when they visited, 'Why are you here?' 'What do you want?' 'Why don't you just go away and never come back, I'm not going to make you welcome anyway!' And he made sure he didn't; so it was only Ian's friends and family that visited.

The loneliness I was now living with was a loneliness within my marriage. Ian and I were not close at all. There were no hugs, no kisses, no intimacy, no sex, no time for each other. We were far from being happy and I could see gaps forming in our marriage.

Unexpectedly I stumbled into a brief glimmer of light. I found myself at the end of yet another tether and I let some of my hurt out in a conversation with Carolyn, a friend at Chapel, she told me she had come through the same tunnel, despite the journey being long.

Strangely enough this was encouragement, and even though things didn't change around me, it helped with how I viewed things.

I hadn't shared my hurt with anyone since the support group ended. Carolyn understood from a position of experience, she had empathy and it showed in her eyes.

This was sad.

But good.

Winter was dragging its feet, and one dark day I found myself on the computer and drawing, I was trying to understand my feelings somehow. I can't draw that well, so my efforts were very poor, but I found it helped me with my baggage of depression, I tried to draw how I pictured my sadness and aloneness.

My first drawing had Ian on one side, standing proud with Anna and James at his feet. Then there was me, in a crumpled heap on the other side of the picture on the floor, with my face in my hands in foetal position almost, some distance from them with darkness all around me.

Drawing helped me express my feelings in a way I'd not considered before.

A number of weeks later spring made a welcome appearance, this meant I was able to spend time outdoors with the kids. We'd be in the garden and I'd leave my phone in the house, I switched it to silent so the calls would go to voice mail, I truly didn't want to speak to anyone. I did my mummy duties – taking Anna to and from the school nursery, looking after James, shopping and cooking, but I spent time outside, it was liberating not to be shut inside the house.

This reflected in my next drawing, it had a bit of hope in it. It had me and the kids in the garden, and the phone switched off so no one could call and ask how I was feeling all the time. And the cat was with us, I'd got a cup of coffee by the garden bench and the colourful spring flowers were bursting into life all around us.

By the time I did my third picture I'd spoken to Carolyn, it had two women, one frail (me) and one a bit stronger (Carolyn). The picture showed me in my diminished state standing with someone that understood. This helped me so much. She'd been there, and what's more she'd escaped her dark tunnel. Knowing someone had survived helped me, and I started to get a little better, slowly but surely. What I didn't know at that time was that this was to be my last picture, I guess there is a time and a season for everything.

But sadly, there was one problem from the pregnancy that didn't seem to be going away, it was the pain in my pelvis, its name is Symphysis Pubis Dysfunction (SPD). I was given a belt to wear, it was like a large tubigrip, it was ok when you first put it on, but each time you moved it rolled and was useless. I'd been to aqua-natal while I was pregnant and physio since the birth, but sadly neither worked for me, though I know for lots of women it works like magic for them, but for me the physio man and the young lady at aqua-natal had no idea what I was struggling with. So when I had an opportunity I talked about my pain with my friend Mary, she is a holistics practitioner. She told me she was studying a new technique called Bowen and asked me if I would like to be a case study, and I said yes.

And that was how my pelvis was fixed.

No stupid belts that never stayed in place, no physio nor aqua-natal carried out by men/women that didn't understand what it was like to suffer such intense pain for so long. Three sessions of a simple technique, and I didn't even have to undress! It worked for me, but it may not work for everyone.

This became a tiny light shining at the end of my tunnel. For the first time in almost a year I was no longer in pain with my pelvis. This meant that when I pushed the buggy up or down the kerb, up or down the steps to the front door, or when I turned over in bed that I didn't wince with pain. That when I got in or out of the bath I didn't have to stand on a child's step, I could behave like an everyday human being, and I didn't need to take pills for the pain any more. This meant so much to me. Being able to speak to people using sentences that made sense because I was getting more sleep and taking less medication. Wow! Almost human!

As I was now a mum of two I decided to change my career; for years I had been a PA at the local solicitor's office and I moved into a part-time teaching job at the local college. Why did I change? Because I couldn't afford to pay child care for two youngsters on my wages and I needed a job with school holidays, Ian would never change jobs to fit in with the children and he'd never pay for child care. I moved to a job where I taught the secretarial and admin skills I had gained over the years, and this brought about a change in me.

A little more confidence, and a little more hope.

That's how it happened.

A little at a time.

But I will never forget the ladies at the postnatal depression support group that met in the back room of the small church just off the main road; although I can't remember their names, and now can't recall their faces, I'll always remember their love and kindness. I'll never forget the feeling of being accepted exactly as I was, and having our names written on the board. We supported each other, because we were all walking the same path. We spoke, we understood, and we cried.

As well as the lady Doctor who was there for me. A working mum, she knows the guilt mums feel when they go out to work and leave their children with a child minder /nursery worker / or at the school gate. She gave me hope.

So, life went on, it slightly improved when the sun shone, and over the next few years I was working full time plus studying part time; I discovered a love for learning and it helped me with my career opportunities. I fitted my study time into the gaps in the marriage and gained a Teaching Qualification and a Degree; sometimes I studied at an evening class, and as I was teaching in a college there were times I'd be teaching on a Saturday morning or on an evening. This meant Ian had the kids and would take them walking round the local lakes or play a game of hide and seek, or he'd take them swimming.

But as I continued to improve I could clearly see that things were getting worse in the relationship of our marriage, so one evening after the kids were asleep I spoke to Ian about my concerns – it had been on my mind for some time – I was being serious but I'm not sure he saw it that way, I said I thought it would be a good move if we went to marriage counselling – Ian laughed in my face, he told me there was nothing wrong with the marriage, he believed that seeing a counsellor was not necessary and we certainly didn't need help from an outsider, and that was all he'd say on the matter as one of his programmes was coming on the TV .. so I left the room, but my concerns continued to grow.

His addiction to the TV, plus his increasing level of control of me and the children, grew and this included what we did on a weekend, how I spent my salary and who I could be with, he controlled everything.

I tried to tell myself I was imagining things, postnatal blues, lack of sleep, new job and all that, I said life would get better soon.

But deep down, I knew I was lying to myself.

How did I come to this? I don't know exactly. I'd got a hubby and two lovely kids, so where were the problems? Well, we had finance worries but who doesn't? I was aware that my salary was larger than his so for the first 10 years of our marriage I paid all the bills. Then as his salary improved (a bit) I chose what I thought was a reasonable moment to ask if he would pay some of the smaller bills (electricity and TV) while I still paid the larger bills (mortgage, gas and Council Tax), he was furious, but I stood my ground and said I couldn't keep paying for everything, he sulked for over a week. It sort-of worked but I found I was often paying more and more if we went out, or when we went to the shops, because when we were in the queue at the till he'd disappear to the toilet, only reappearing when I had paid for the shopping. But I cottoned on to this behaviour and would wait for him to come back so he could take his turn paying.

But then there were other things, such as the way he stared at other women everywhere we went (even when he was driving) I always felt I was never good enough for him, I certainly wasn't his one and only. I'd see him when we were on holiday (always self-catering – even our honeymoon was self-catering!), I saw him arm in arm with a dolly-bird on more than one occasion, he'd deny everything of course, but I'm not stupid, I knew I'd seen him. He was never faithful, he never looked after me for better, it was always worse, he never looked after me in sickness nor in health, he never loved or cherished me, and never ever kept a solemn vow!

And then there was his constant habit of changing the subject when I got too close in a conversation and he wanted to hide something. His behaviour had changed over the years, he became a controller, of everything that he could control, and of some things he shouldn't. He controlled things ranging from who me and the kids could see, through to the pocket money the kids were given by other people, Ian would make sure the kids spent their pocket money on food. At Christmas his dad would send a cheque for the kids, but it would only be made out to Ian – it was like I didn't exist! So I opened a small joint account at the bank, I had this set up specifically to put the cheque in so the kids would get the Christmas money spent on them. He would raid their piggy banks, saying 'I need change to park the car, I'll put it back' but he never did. He would get me to pay for things needed for the house, such as wall paper, paint, tiles for the bathroom, carpets and furniture, always promising to pay half, but he never did. He knew I wouldn't ask him for the money.

And there was something else, something had been brewing, and for a long time I couldn't put my finger on it. I'm not sure when it happened but it slowly dawned on me that I was completely and utterly afraid of Ian. He seemed to exude rage somehow, and he frightened me. This affected me in an unexpected and very deep way. I was being mentally controlled and abused, I became afraid to speak freely, certainly too afraid to argue – I wouldn't dare to disagree with him.

So as time went on, me and the kids played a game called keeping daddy happy. Because if he was happy there was no shouting. Because when the shouting started it was quickly followed by smacking. And Ian didn't have a stop button once he started smacking. I had to pull him off the children. I'd hold them as their sobs subsided, and then I'd see to the welts where he had smacked unceasingly.

Ian never knew how to play with the children. He Always Had To Win! He couldn't ever lose. No matter if it was a board game, rough and tumble, football or cards. With every game he had a single focus of winning no matter what. He loved winning even it if meant him changing the rules. With rough and tumble he would hold the children down until they were crying for him to release them. I'd be shouting at him and telling him he was hurting them, that rough and tumble was only a game and he shouldn't be such a bully, but he was deaf to me, singularly focused on overpowering them and getting them to plead for mercy, he wouldn't stop until he forced them to say he had won and that they surrendered.

I'd then be left with a traumatised and bruised child.

My love for him died.

His behaviour affected me and the kids badly; the mental abuse we were suffering was a daily onslaught, but it was in the dark of the night, when the nightmares came, that was the worst time of all.

As well as his controlling and bullying behaviour I had my suspicions there were other abuses going on in the house, but I was too afraid to admit them, even to myself.

Ian had a few 'night antics' and one was getting up and going to the bathroom during the night, nothing strange in that, I'll admit – but there were often times I'd hear him go downstairs and switch the TV on. One morning over breakfast I asked him why he did this and he said he needed to program the TV to record something, so I left it at that – for a while, but there was something in his manner that made me not believe him. So, one night when he went downstairs I crept down after him, and I caught him watching porn. He apologised, and then said something very odd, he insisted on going to speak to the Pastor at Chapel to confess. I was surprised at this because confession is not something we do at Chapel. I guess he saw this as a secondary way of using porn as our Pastor is a woman.

I also caught him out having viewed porn sites on the computer.

With these (and other) events he was always sorry and promised his behaviour would improve, and sometimes it seemed to, for a couple of weeks or so, and then his habits would slowly creep back.

Any feelings I had for him were diminishing at a rapid rate of knots, and my loveless sexless marriage of over 10 years had ground itself to a halt and was stuck in a rut. I was at a loss as to what I should do with it or about it, and I wasn't even sure if I wanted to bother. I felt suicidal and often wanted to run away. I had a spot in the hills I would sometimes escape to so that I could cry, get angry and scream it all out before going back home.

But at least the children were growing and flourishing, and by the time the next season happened both were at senior school.

*